Wanted

WANTED

Kings and Priests

Rooted in Identity, Formed in Faith

Tiffany K. Grainger

CROWN & ALTAR
PUBLISHING

COPYRIGHT PAGE

Wanted
Kings and Priests

Copyright © 2025 by **Tiffany K. Grainger**

Scripture Quotations

Published by
Crown & Altar Publishing
Pueblo | Colorado | U.S.A.

ISBN (Paperback): 979-8-9951024-0-3
ISBN (eBook): 979-8-9951024-1-0

Cover design by: Crown & Altar Publishing
Interior design by: Crown & Altar Publishing

Printed in the United States of America

First Edition

Legal Disclaimer

This book is intended for inspirational and educational purposes
only. It is not a substitute for professional counseling, medical, or
legal advice. The author and publisher are not liable for any
actions taken based on the contents of this book.

Dedication

To my family, for a lifetime of love, support and encouragement.

To my husband and children, for your love, patience, and constant encouragement.

To my pastors, for your faithful leadership and steady example.

And above all:
To God the Father, for loving me before I knew what true love meant; to Jesus Christ, for Your sacrifice and redeeming grace; and to the Holy Spirit, for Your constant encouragement and guidance in every word written here.

All glory belongs to God.

Table of Contents

Authors Note

For the sake of clarity, I use Biblical terms such as "kings" and "priests" throughout this book. These roles apply equally to men and women in Christ, and any masculine language is intended to include all, not to exclude.

Part I: Identity

Before responsibility comes identity.

Before calling comes belonging.

Part I lays the foundation for everything that follows. It addresses the quiet, but defining question beneath so many struggles: *Who am I, really?*

In these chapters, you will explore what it means to be wanted before redemption, intentional rather than accidental, known and named by God, and not an afterthought in His story. This section confronts the subtle beliefs many of us carry: that we are tolerated rather than desired, saved reluctantly rather than pursued with love.

Identity is not something we construct; it is something we receive. When that foundation is unstable, everything built upon it feels fragile. However, when identity is anchored in truth, responsibility becomes steady and intimacy becomes natural.

Before you learn how to walk as a king and priest, you must first understand who you are.

This is where that understanding begins.

Chapter 1:
Wanted

What do you think of, when you think of the word "wanted?" For some, a Western movie might pop into their head, with a "Wanted" poster of the bad guy where there's a reward out for his capture. For others they think about something they desired to have as a child. Yet others might experience a sharp sense of "something I'll never be" and still others might think about a job, a car, a home or something else they would have liked to have.

In this chapter, we are going to define "wanted" as: desired, needed, sought after, required, intended, planned, chosen, and cared for. Think about this for a moment: Before you were redeemed, you were *wanted, desired, needed, chosen, planned.*

What was your first thought when you read that? Did you immediately reject it? Did you question it? Did you accept it? That sentence challenges many of the assumptions Christians quietly live with. We are comfortable saying God *saved* us. We are less comfortable believing He *wanted* us. Yet Scripture tells us plainly that God's love did not begin at the Cross, it preceded it. *"Even before he made the world, God loved us and chose us in Christ to be holy and without fault in his eyes. God decided in advance to adopt us into his own family by bringing us to himself through Jesus Christ. This is what he wanted to do, and it gave him great pleasure."* (Ephesians 1:4-5, NLT). Long before there was sin to forgive, there was desire. Long before redemption was necessary, love was already present.

Somewhere along the way, many of us absorbed the idea that God rescued us reluctantly. That we were a problem that He chose to fix, rather than a person He longed to love. We learned to see ourselves as tolerated, not treasured. Forgiven, but not enjoyed. However, that story does not begin where the Bible begins.

Think about it for a moment. Scripture opens not with redemption, but with intention. Before there was ever sin to forgive, there was a God who chose to create. Before there was brokenness to heal, there was a deliberate act of love that said, *Let there be man.* Creation itself is evidence of desire. You exist because God wanted you to exist. Not as an experiment. Not as an afterthought. *"So God created man in his own image, in the image of God created he him; male and female created he them"* (Genesis 1:27, KJV). God did not create reluctantly. He created deliberately and He called what He made good. You were created because it pleased Him to create you and sin did not erase that desire. When Adam and Eve fell, God did not step back and reconsider His decision. He did not decide we were a mistake and only worth salvaging out of obligation. He moved toward us. He sought. He pursued. He promised redemption, not because He suddenly discovered our worth, but because He never lost sight of it. Scripture tells us that *"God clearly shows and proves His own love for us, by the fact that while we were still sinners, Christ died for us."* (Romans 5:8, AMP). Redemption was not God changing His mind about us. Redemption was God refusing to give up on what He had already called good.

We often reverse the order in our thinking. We assume we became valuable *after* Jesus died for us. However, Scripture tells a different story: *"Long ago the LORD said to Israel: "I have loved you, my people, with an everlasting love. With unfailing love I have drawn you to myself"* (Jeremiah 31:3, NLT). Everlasting means without beginning and without end. Jesus came because we were already valuable to the Father. No one gives their most precious gift for something they consider worthless. The Cross does not prove our worthlessness, it reveals our worth. This is where many believers struggle. We have been taught; sometimes explicitly, sometimes subtly, that seeing ourselves as valuable is dangerous; that it leads to pride. That humility requires us to see ourselves as lowly, insignificant, and undeserving. However, humility is not denying what God declares. Humility is agreeing with God even when it challenges our self-concept. *"For God so loved the world that he gave his one and only Son, that whoever believes in him shall not perish but have eternal life"* (John 3:16, NIV). Love is the motive. Love always was.

If God says you are wanted, rejecting that is not humility, it is disbelief. Being desired by God does not make us arrogant. It makes us secure and secure people are not driven by comparison, jealousy, or fear. They are free to love, to serve, and to obey without needing to prove themselves. We must be careful not to confuse grace with disdain. Grace does not mean God rescued us because He felt sorry for us. Grace means God acted on our behalf because love compelled Him to do so. Grace flows from affection, not pity. Yes, we were sinners. Sin was real. Separation was real. The cost of redemption was real. However, sin was never the truest thing about you.

The truth is:

- You were a child before you were a sinner.
- You were desired before you were lost.
- You were known before you were redeemed.

When we start from the wrong foundation, when we believe we were only ever a problem to be solved, we will live like spiritual orphans even while claiming the name of Christ. We will obey out of fear instead of love. We will settle for survival instead of sonship. We will struggle to believe that God delights in us.

When we begin with desire, everything shifts. If God wanted you before you ever responded to Him, then your worth is not fragile. It does not rise and fall with your performance. It is not erased by failure or diminished by weakness. You are not on probation with God. You are not an unwanted guest in His Kingdom. You are His idea and He does not regret His ideas.

This does not minimize repentance, it deepens it. When we understand that we were desired, repentance stops being driven by shame and starts being driven by relationship. We turn back to God not because we fear rejection, but because we trust His heart.

To be wanted by God is not sentimental. It is transformative.

- It changes how we pray.
- It changes how we endure suffering.
- It changes how we see ourselves (and others).

It also prepares us for the truth that comes next: if we are wanted children, then we are also called to live as kings and priests, not striving for identity, but standing firmly in it.

Before you were redeemed, you were desired and that truth changes everything.

Reflection Questions:
Wanted

1. When you hear the statement *"Before I was redeemed, I was desired,"* what is your immediate reaction: agreement, discomfort, resistance, or confusion? Why do you think that is?

2. If you grew up in faith (or around faith), what messages did you absorb, explicitly or implicitly, about why God saved you? If you did not grow up in or around faith, what messages did you absorb, explicitly or implicitly, about God in general (kind and loving or perhaps angry deity ready to strike you down or maybe something else)?

3. Do you tend to picture God as eager to have you, or reluctant, but gracious? How does that picture affect the way you relate to Him?

4. Have you ever believed, consciously or unconsciously, that God loves you *because He has to*, rather than because He wants to? Or perhaps you've believed that God doesn't love you at all. How have these beliefs shaped your prayer life or obedience?

5. The chapter talks about how creation itself is evidence of God's desire. What would it mean for you personally if your existence was not accidental, but intentional and pleasing to God?

6. Which feels harder for you to accept:

   o That God forgives you, or

   o That God delights in you?

Why do you think that is?

7. How might your understanding of humility need to shift if humility means agreeing with God about who you are, rather than minimizing yourself?

8. In what ways have you tied your worth to performance, obedience, or spiritual success instead of God's original desire for you?

9. If you truly believed that God wanted you *before* you ever responded to Him, how might that change the way you view your failures or weaknesses?

10. Take a moment of quiet and ask God this question:
"Did You want me?"
Write down whatever comes to mind, without correcting, dismissing, or theologizing it away.

Before you move on, sit with this truth. Don't rush past it. Identity does not form through speed, but through agreement. Let yourself consider (perhaps for the first time) that you were wanted. What does that mean and how does that change things in your life?

Chapter 2:
Priceless

Let me challenge you with a question:

What would change in your life if you truly believed that God actually wanted you?

You are not a mistake. You are not an accident. You are not an unwanted child God somehow ended up with. You are intentional. You are created. You are priceless.

How would your life change if you truly believed that—and lived accordingly?

So many of us carry a quiet weight. We believe lies we would never say out loud: *I'm not special. I'll never be enough. God saved me because no one else would want me. I keep messing up, why even try?* We dress these lies up as humility, but they are still lies.

God speaks something entirely different:

You are loved. You are wanted. You are precious.

God did not save you out of pity. He did not rescue you as a favor. He sent His only Son because of the deep value He placed on you. No one pays the highest price for something they consider worthless.

We forget that the God who redeemed us is the God who first created us and He does not regret His creation. Many believers quietly assume that God created humanity in general and then figured out the details later. However, Scripture tells us otherwise. *You formed my inward parts; You knit me together in my mother's womb… all the days ordained for me were written in Your book before one of them came to be"* (Psalm 139:13,16, NIV).

Have you ever made something with your own hands? One year, my husband and I took a pottery class together. As I carefully shaped the clay, I couldn't help but think of how intentionally God forms each of us. My bowls weren't perfect. Others might not have valued them at all, but to me they were precious because I had made them. When I returned to pick them up, one of my pieces was gone. It had cracked in the kiln, and the owner assumed I wouldn't want it. I was devastated. Even broken, it still mattered to me.

That is how God sees us. Even when the world calls us flawed, cracked, or disposable, God never stops calling us His. We may feel broken, but He still sees the beauty of His design and He loves us for who we are.

So I'll ask again:

What would change if you truly believed God wanted you?

When I begin to believe that God wants me, my entire outlook shifts. I don't just have a purpose, I exist because God desired me. Grace did not erase my value; it was given because of it.

I walk with confidence, not pride, because I am a child of the King. I obey, not out of fear or obligation, but out of love. I stop speaking death over myself, because it contradicts what my Father says is true. Biblical humility is not thinking less of yourself, it is agreeing with God. False humility denies what God declares. True humility receives identity as a gift, not an achievement.

Yes, we were sinners and yes, we were saved by grace; however, sin was never our identity; it was our condition. Grace did not make us valuable. Grace restored us to relationship with the God who already valued us. Identity shapes behavior. When we live like beloved children, we stop crawling in the mud of shame and start walking in the authority we were given.

Jesus said, *"Do not be afraid; only believe."* (Mark 5:36b, NKJV). Belief, true belief, changes everything.

Reflection Questions:
Priceless

1. When you hear the word *priceless*, do you instinctively apply it to yourself? Why or why not?

2. What beliefs have shaped your sense of worth: family messages, past failures, cultural expectations, spiritual teaching?

3. Do you tend to measure your value by performance, productivity, or obedience? How has that influenced your relationship with God?

4. The chapter discusses how grace did not create your value, but revealed it. How does that challenge or reshape the way you think about salvation?

5. Have you ever believed that God saved you out of obligation rather than desire? What evidence do you hold for that belief?

6. How does the image of being intentionally formed; known before you were born, affect the way you see your past, including your wounds or weaknesses?

7. What lies about your worth do you quietly repeat that you might never say out loud?

8. If you truly believed you were priceless to God, what would change in:

   o   The way you speak about yourself?

   o   The way you handle failure?

   o   The way you pursue obedience?

9. Does accepting your value feel uncomfortable or prideful to you? Why do you think humility and worth sometimes feel opposed?

10. Sit quietly and ask:
    "Father, where have I undervalued what You call precious?"
    Write down what surfaces without filtering or correcting it.

Chapter 3:
Which Tap Are You Opening?

Imagine stepping into the shower and seeing two handles connected to the same faucet. Both are within reach. Both are available. You turn the handle on the right, and clear, clean water pours out; pure and refreshing. Then you turn the handle on the left and dirty, brown sludge begins to flow.

Which one would you choose?

The answer seems obvious. Most of us would never willingly bathe in filth when clean water is available and yet, spiritually, we do this all the time. When we came to Christ, when we believed that Jesus is the Son of God, that He died for our sins and rose again, we opened the tap to the blessings that come with accepting all that God did for us. Forgiveness, freedom, peace, healing, wisdom, and hope became ours. The old life, marked by separation and death, no longer had authority over us.

But too often, we open the other tap.

We begin to speak words that contradict what God has said: *I'm not worth it. I'll always struggle. Nothing good ever happens to me. I'm sick. I'm broken. I'm not enough.* and while the clean water is still flowing, we are allowing it to be mixed with sludge.

Then we stand under the stream and wonder why life feels heavy. Why joy feels distant. Why peace seems elusive. The problem is not that the clean water stopped flowing. The problem is that we opened both taps. God's truth has not failed us. His presence has not left us. His promises have not disappeared., but when we continually open ourselves to fear, shame, self-pity, and hopelessness, we allow those things to contaminate what God is pouring into our lives.

If you fill a bathtub with sludge, you will bathe in sludge. It doesn't matter how much clean water you allow in afterward. If you want the water to be clean, turning off the dirty tap is necessary, but it isn't enough. The sludge that has already accumulated must be drained out and the clean water must be the only thing that is allowed to flow. This is where many believers get discouraged. They begin speaking truth. They start declaring God's promises, but when everything doesn't immediately change, they assume it isn't working. So, they return to old patterns of thinking and speaking, reopening the tap they had just closed and sludge pours back in.

Please keep in mind that turning off the sludge tap does not mean ignoring trauma, denying grief, or pretending pain isn't real. Healing is often slow and layered, but God is patient, gentle, and present in the process. This is not about blame, it is about hope. Remember, cleansing takes time. If you have ever tried to wash dirt out of a container by running clean water through it, you know this is true. At first, the water looks cloudy. The dirt swirls around. It may even seem worse before it gets better. However, if the clean water keeps flowing, and no more dirt is added, the dirt eventually washes out completely.

Once it's gone, stirring the water doesn't make it dirty again (unless you introduce new dirt). Our lives work the same way. When we consistently choose truth over lies, faith over fear, and

God's voice over our own accusations, the sludge begins to drain. It may not happen overnight, but it *will* happen, if we stay steadfast. The problem is not the presence of old sludge. The problem is reopening the sludge tap. When anxiety, anger, despair, or self-condemnation dominate our thoughts and words, we are not uncovering God's absence, we are revealing where our focus has gone. God has not left. His clean water has not stopped flowing. It is there and will always be there, as long as we leave that tap open, but if we don't shut off the sludge we will struggle to see the clean, clear water.

This is not a promise that life will be easy or free from hardship. Jesus never taught that. The clean water of God's truth does not eliminate storms, it anchors us in them. Faith is not pretending pain doesn't exist; it is refusing to let pain define who God is or who we are. Our words do not control God, but they do reveal what we are agreeing with. When our speech aligns with God's truth, we position ourselves to live from faith rather than fear. This is not about commanding God; it is about refusing to partner with lies.

What this is and what it is not:

- This is not denying that suffering can occur.
- This is not trying to earn God's favor (you already have it).
- This is not pretending life is perfect.
- This is: choosing truth over lies.
- This is: learning to live from identity instead of fear.
- This is: refusing to call unclean what God has called clean.

The invitation is simple, but not easy: **Shut off the sludge tap. Open the drain. Keep the clean water flowing** and when the dirt tries to swirl back up, stand firm. Jesus said, *"Do not be afraid; only believe."* (Mark 5:36).

Belief determines which tap you turn.

Reflection Questions:
Which Tap Are You Opening?

1. When you think about God, do you believe He merely tolerates you or that He genuinely wants you? What experiences or teachings have shaped that belief?

2. What "sludge tap" do you find yourself opening most often?
   (Fear, self-criticism, anxiety, hopelessness, anger, comparison, shame, or something else?)

3. What phrases or thoughts do you commonly speak over yourself that may contradict what God says is true about you?

4. How do you usually respond when life feels heavy or circumstances don't change quickly, do you remain rooted in truth, or do you return to old patterns of thinking?

5. In what ways might your daily decisions, relationships, or prayers look different if you truly believed you are deeply wanted and valued by God?

6. Are there areas of your life where you've closed the sludge tap but haven't yet allowed the "drain" to run, places where old beliefs, wounds, or habits still linger?

7. What would it look like, practically, to keep the clean water flowing this week?
   (Consider your thoughts, words, time with God, or the voices you allow to influence you.)

8. When you experience fear or discouragement, how might Jesus' words, *"Do not be afraid; only believe"* change the way you respond?

9. Do you believe that choosing truth is an act of humility rather than pride? Why or why not?

10. Take a moment to ask God this simple question:
    "What do You want me to know about how You see me?"
    Write down what comes to mind without editing or dismissing it

Belief is not proven by what we say once, it is revealed by what we return to again and again. Pay attention this week to which tap you open, and trust that God is patient as you learn to live from truth.

Chapter 4:
Not an Afterthought

In the last chapter, we talked about being wanted and what that means. This chapter goes deeper into this. Many believers can accept that God loves them in a broad, general sense. What feels harder to believe is that God was intentional about them; that their personality, story, limitations, and place in history were not accidents to be managed, but designs to be fulfilled.

We often imagine God creating humanity in bulk and then dealing with the details later, as if we were the result of a divine production line rather than a deliberate act of craftsmanship. However, Scripture does not support that idea. God does not improvise. You were not born because God needed more people. You were born because God intended *you*. *"Before I formed you in the womb, I knew you"* (Jeremiah 1:5a, NIV).

Knowledge preceded formation and intention preceded existence. The God who wanted you is the God who formed you. He did not simply decide that the world needed more people. He decided that the world needed *you*. Your life did not begin as a contingency plan or a secondary option. You were not born because God ran out of better ideas.

You were never an afterthought.

When Samuel stood before Jesse's sons, David wasn't even in the room. He was still in the field. He was overlooked by his own father and brothers. If God worked the way we sometimes imagine, Samuel would have just chosen from the sons who were presented to him. He even told God, "Hey, Eliab looks like he's perfect!" *"When they arrived, Samuel saw Eliab and thought, "Surely the Lord's anointed stands here before the Lord."* (1 Samuel 16:6, NLT). Samuel saw Eliab and, from man's perspective, he looked good. *"But the Lord said to Samuel, "Do not consider his appearance or his height, for I have rejected him. The Lord does not look at the things people look at. People look at the outward appearance, but the Lord looks at the heart."* (1 Samuel 16:7 NLT). God did not adjust His plan to fit appearances. He did not scan the room and settle for the best available option. He called for the overlooked one. He was not adjusting to circumstances or improvising. Before Samuel ever poured oil over David's head, before David faced Goliath, before he wrote a single psalm, God had already chosen him. David might have been an afterthought to his family, but he was not an afterthought to God; he was the intention.

From the very beginning, God has worked with specificity. He names. He calls. He assigns purpose before action. He speaks identity before behavior. This is true throughout Scripture and it is true of you. Long before you made a single decision, God knew you. Before you developed strengths or weaknesses, He saw you. Before you succeeded or failed, He chose to create you exactly as you are.

This does not mean hardship was authored by God. It means no hardship has disqualified you from His purpose. *"My counsel shall stand, and I will accomplish all My purpose"* (Isaiah 46:10, ESV). Too many Christians carry the quiet belief that they were created despite their flaws, rather than with full knowledge of them. We imagine

God sighing over our weaknesses and constantly adjusting His plans to accommodate our mistakes. However, an all-knowing God does not improvise. He was not surprised by your temperament. He was not caught off guard by your struggles. He was not disappointed with your perceived limitations. Scripture tells us, *"For we are His workmanship, created in Christ Jesus for good works, which God prepared beforehand so that we would walk in them"* (Ephesians 2:10, NASB 1995). Prepared beforehand means nothing about your life is accidental.

God does not create and then react. He creates with knowledge and purpose. If your life feels messy or unfinished, that does not mean it is accidental. It means it is still in process. We tend to look at our present circumstances and conclude that something must have gone wrong. However, intention does not always look like clarity, especially in the middle of becoming who we were truly supposed to be.

The Bible is not filled with flawless people placed neatly into perfect roles. It is filled with unlikely individuals, complicated stories, and slow unfolding purpose. God does not rush identity and He does not abandon design. You do not need to prove that your life makes sense in order for it to be meaningful. Your life is meaningful because the Creator of the Universe created you with meaning and purpose. Being "not an afterthought" also means that you were not created to fill space or play a background role in God's kingdom. There are no filler people in the body of Christ. No expendable lives. No one whose presence is optional. Each and every person who has ever been created and who ever will be created has a purpose (even those who deny this truth). Some choose to not fulfill their purpose. Some choose to deny that they have purpose. Some choose to believe that their purpose is minimal or nonexistent. None of this changes the fact that you were created for a plan and purpose and that the Creator of the Universe formed you, created you, and wanted you. If you choose to not believe this, then you can easily fall into the trap of believing that you are replaceable and comparison thrives when we believe we are replaceable. However, intentional design eliminates comparison. When you understand that God formed you on purpose, you no longer need to compete for significance, as the Bible says, *"The steps of a man are ordered by the LORD who takes delight in his journey."* (Proverbs 16:9, BSB). Your role is not diminished by someone else's calling. You are not behind. You are not late. You are not disqualified. You are not replaceable. You are essential. You are valuable. You have a purpose.

God's intention for your life did not begin when you first believed. It does not activate when you get things right. It existed before you were aware of it and it continues even when you struggle to see it. Being "not an afterthought" means you can stop striving to justify your existence.

- You do not need to earn your place.
- You do not need to validate your worth.
- You do not need to apologize for taking up space in God's story.

You are here because God intended you to be and intention, once established by God, is not undone by human weakness. This truth prepares us for what comes next. If we were intentionally formed, then our identity carries responsibility. We were not just created to exist, we were created to represent. Kings and priests are not accidental roles. They require intention and so do you.

Reflection Questions:
Not an Afterthought

1. When you consider your life story, do you tend to see it as intentional or accidental? What moments or experiences have shaped that perception?

2. The chapter states that God does not create and then react. How does that challenge the way you've understood God's involvement in your life?

3. Are there parts of yourself; your personality, struggles, past, or limitations that you have assumed God must be constantly "working around" rather than intentionally allowing? Why?

4. How do you usually respond when your life feels messy, unclear, or unfinished? Do you interpret that as failure, delay, or process?

5. In what ways has comparison influenced how you see your value or role in God's kingdom? How might believing you are not replaceable change that?

6. Do you believe there are "filler people" in God's story, including yourself? Where did that belief come from?

7. What would it look like to trust that your life is still unfolding according to God's intention, even if you don't yet see how the pieces fit together?

8. How might your relationship with God shift if you believed He was not disappointed by your limitations or surprised by your struggles?

9. Are there areas where you feel pressure to justify your existence; to prove your worth, calling, or usefulness? What would it feel like to release that pressure?

10. Sit quietly with this statement and reflect on it:
    "I am not an afterthought in God's story."
    What resistance, comfort, or questions does it stir in you?

As you continue, resist the urge to rush ahead. Identity unfolds best when it is received, not forced.

Chapter 5:
Known and Named

As a college professor, on the very first day of class, I ask my students to introduce themselves. I also give them a paper nameplate and ask them to write their names in bold letters. Why? Because I care about learning who they are. Imagine if, four weeks into the semester, I stood at the front of the room and said, "Hey, you, come up here." The room would go quiet. Eyes would drop. Students would suddenly become very interested in their notebooks, their phones, or the floor. It would be awkward and uncomfortable.

Instead, I call on my students by name. "Emma, would you help me pass these out?" "Brandon, I would love to hear your thoughts on this." When a name is spoken, something shifts. When someone knows they have been seen, truly seen, something changes.

Over the years, I have had students take one class with me and then return to take another class and another, semester after semester. As I came to know them more personally, the conversations change. I was no longer just calling on a name; I was speaking from relationship. "Emma, I know you might hesitate before you speak, but you see things others miss." "Brandon, you think deeply and share meaningful insight." As that happened, something else shifted, they stepped forward with greater boldness, they spoke up a little sooner, they expressed themselves with more confidence.

Knowing their names made a difference. Knowing them as a person made an even greater difference. Scripture reveals a God who does not issue vague invitations into a crowd, hoping someone qualified might volunteer. He calls by name. He knows before He sends. He speaks identity before responsibility.

When Jesus called Simon "Peter," He was not hoping Simon would someday become steady. He was speaking from knowledge, not wishful thinking. When God renamed Abram "Abraham," it was not motivational language. It was revelation. To be known by God means you are not interchangeable. You are not one of many hoping the assignment might apply to you. When He calls, He is not experimenting. He is inviting. When you understand that, you see the calling and the partnership He desires to have with you.

To be wanted tells us something about God's heart. To be intentional tells us something about God's design. To be known tells us something about God's relationship with us. God does not love humanity in theory while remaining distant from individuals. He does not relate to us as a giant group, He knows us personally and He always has. The Bible repeatedly reveals a God who names before He sends, who knows before He calls, and who establishes identity before responsibility. Being known by God is not a future reward for faithfulness; it is the starting point of relationship.

Long before you learned how to describe yourself, God already knew you.

- He knew your thoughts before you thought them.
- He knew your days before you lived them.

- He knew your strengths, your fears, your questions, and your potential.

This kind of knowledge is not observational, it is relational, *"Fear not, for I have redeemed you; I have called you by name, you are mine"* (Isaiah 43:1b, ESV).

To be known by God means you are not interchangeable. You are not one of many indistinguishable believers fulfilling a general role. Before you were ever born, before you ever said a word, God already knew you and He still knows you. He knows you more deeply than you might know or understand. He knows the words you will speak and the heart with which you speak them, *"You know what I am going to say even before I say it, LORD"* (Psalm 139:4, NLT). He knows you intimately, *"I know My own and My own know Me"* (John 10:14b, ESV). God's knowledge of you is personal, specific, and complete and with that knowledge comes naming.

Throughout Scripture, when God names someone (or renames them) it is never casual. Names are not labels; they are declarations. They reveal calling, identity, and destiny.

- Abram became Abraham before the promise was fulfilled. (Genesis 17:5).

- Jacob became Israel before his character fully reflected it. (Genesis 32:28).

- Simon was called Peter long before he became steadfast. (Matthew 16:18).

God names people not according to who they have been, but according to who they are becoming. To be named by God is to be invited into agreement with Him. This is where the shift begins, if God knows you personally and names you purposefully, then your life is not merely about personal growth or private faith. It is about the responsibility you have to carry out the plans and purposes He has for your life. As the Bible says, *"But now that you know God—or rather are known by God—how is it that you are turning back to those weak and miserable forces? Do you wish to be enslaved by them all over again?"* (Galatians 4:9, NIV). Identity carries responsibility.

Relationship leads to representation. Representation leads to glory to God and fulfilling His plans.

In Scripture, those who are known by God are entrusted with authority.

- Priests were known before they were appointed.
- Kings were named before they were crowned.

They were not chosen because they were impressive; they were entrusted because they were called.

- ❖ Kingship in the kingdom of God is not about dominance, it is about stewardship. It is the responsibility to represent God's Kingdom with wisdom, justice, and humility.
- ❖ Priesthood is not about religious performance, it is about access. Priests stand before God on behalf of others and before others on behalf of God. They carry presence, not pretense.

Both roles require identity before function.

We struggle with standing in our authority when we do not believe we are known. We resist responsibility when we doubt that God understands who we truly are. However, when we are secure in being known and named, we no longer fear being sent and we no longer cower in the winepress, hiding from perceived enemies (Judges 6-8). When we understand that God has named us and that we are known and loved by Him, we recognize that He does not assign roles randomly. He entrusts them relationally. To be known and named means you are not only loved, you are called. When you see you are called, you will realize that calling is not something you invent; it is something you receive. You do not have to strive for significance when God has already spoken it over you. You do not have to prove your worth before stepping into responsibility. You live from your identity in Christ, not in a constant striving toward whatever you think that identity is "supposed" to look like.

- ❖ Being known by God anchors us.
- ❖ Being named by God commissions us.

This is the beginning of kingship and priesthood; not as titles to chase, but as identities to inhabit.

Once you truly receive and accept your identity in Christ, authority can be exercised without fear.

Reflection Questions:
Known & Named

1. Do you tend to think of God as knowing people in general, or knowing *you* personally? What makes that distinction difficult or meaningful for you?

2. How does the idea that God knew you before you knew yourself affect the way you view your past, including your mistakes and struggles?

3. When you think about being fully known by God, does that feel comforting, unsettling, or both? Why?

4. Throughout Scripture, God often names or renames people before they live up to that name. Where might God be calling you something you do not yet feel ready to believe?

5. Have you ever resisted the idea of calling or responsibility because you doubted that God truly understood you? What fears are connected to that resistance?

6. The chapter suggests that identity precedes authority. How have you seen the opposite play out, either in yourself or others, when authority is pursued without secure identity?

7. Which role feels more natural for you to accept right now: being *known* by God, or being *named* and entrusted by Him? Why do you think that is?

8. How might your understanding of kingship change if authority is rooted in stewardship rather than power or control?

9. How might your understanding of priesthood change if it is about access and presence rather than performance?

10. Sit quietly and reflect on this question:
    "What name or calling might God be speaking over me that I have been hesitant to receive?"
    Write down what comes to mind, even if it feels incomplete or uncertain.

Before God sends us, He knows us. Before He entrusts us, He names us. Sit with what it means to be known and called; not someday, but now.

Part II: Calling

Identity is not the destination. It is the foundation.

Once you understand who you are, the question naturally shifts: *What am I entrusted with?* Calling is not about striving for significance; it is about stewarding what has already been placed in your hands.

In these chapters, you will explore what it means to live as both king and priest; to carry authority without arrogance and intimacy without withdrawal. You will discover that kingship is rooted in stewardship, not control, and that priesthood is rooted in access, not performance.

Calling is not something you manufacture. It flows from identity. When you know who you are, responsibility no longer feels like pressure, it becomes purpose.

You were not created merely to exist. You were created to represent.

This section invites you to step into that responsibility with clarity and courage.

Chapter 6:
Kings: Authority & Stewardship

Being a king sounds powerful, but what does that truly mean? If I am a king, what kind of authority do I actually carry and how am I meant to use it?

When we hear the word king, we might imagine a throne, a crown, and a kingdom spread out before us. Maybe we picture power, command, and authority exercised from a place of elevation. Except, the first human being that was given authority on Earth did not sit on a throne. He stood in a garden. Before there was ever a monarchy in Israel, before crowns were forged or palaces built, God gave humanity dominion. What did that dominion look like? It looked like tending to what God had created. Naming animals. Guarding what had been entrusted to him. Cultivating life. Adam's authority was not domination; it was stewardship.

He was not told, "Rule for your own glory." He was told to tend and keep the garden. The Hebrew words imply guarding and cultivating. His kingship was expressed not in taking, but in caring. Not in control, but in responsibility. That is the pattern. Biblical authority does not begin with a throne; it begins with trust. It begins with something placed in your hands and the question: Will you steward this well?

Adam was given responsibility before recognition. Authority looked like showing up daily, tending to what God had created, and protecting what God had declared good. This is the kind of kingship we are called into. Not ruling from a distance, but standing faithfully within what has been entrusted to us.

When Scripture calls us kings, it is not giving us a title to admire, it is entrusting us with responsibility. Many believers struggle with the idea of spiritual authority. Some reject it outright, afraid it sounds prideful or dangerous. Others misunderstand it, assuming authority means control, power, or exemption from suffering. The reality is that Biblical kingship looks nothing like worldly dominance. From the very beginning, authority was part of God's design for humanity, *"And God said, 'Let us make man in our image, after our likeness: and let them have dominion over the fish of the sea, and over the fowl of the air, and over the cattle, and over all the earth, and over every creeping thing that creepeth upon the earth.'"* (Genesis 1:26, KJV). Dominion was not domination, it was stewardship. Humanity was entrusted with responsibility, before sin ever entered the world.

Authority, then, is not a reward for maturity. It is part of our original calling. However, in the kingdom of God, authority is never given for self-exaltation. It is given for stewardship. A king in God's design is not defined by how much he takes, but by how faithfully he tends what has been entrusted to him. Authority is not about ruling *over* people, it is about representing God *for* them. Yet many believers are uncomfortable with the idea of authority. We associate it with abuse, pride, or control, but Scripture defines authority differently. Jesus said, *"Whoever wants to become great among you must be your servant"* (Mark 10:43, NIV). In God's kingdom, authority is exercised through faithfulness, humility, and care.

From the beginning, God's intention for humanity included stewardship. Humanity was given responsibility, before it was given redemption. Authority was part of our original design, not a later reward. To be a king, then, is to accept responsibility.

You have authority in places you may not recognize:

- Over the way you respond to circumstances.
- Over what you agree with in your thoughts.
- Over the atmosphere you cultivate in your home.
- Over how you treat others.
- Over how you steward the gifts, resources, and relationships entrusted to you.

Kings do not abdicate responsibility because conditions are difficult. They lead faithfully within those difficult circumstances. Authority does not mean you control outcomes. It means you are accountable for obedience and effective stewardship. This is where many of us hesitate. We fear that accepting authority means accepting blame. We accept the lie that accepting authority is prideful. We would rather see ourselves as powerless than risk failure, but the reality is that refusing responsibility does not produce humility, it produces passivity.

God does not call us to be kings so we can dominate, He calls us kings so we can stand and steward.

- Kings stand in truth when lies press in.
- Kings stand in integrity when compromise seems easier.
- Kings stand in faith when fear feels louder.
- Kings steward resources with care.
- Kings (at least good ones) steward people with love.

Biblical authority is exercised first inwardly and with the little things, before it is ever seen outwardly and with the bigger things. This is demonstrated throughout scripture, such as in Matthew

25:21 (NLT), *"The master said, 'Well done, my good and faithful servant. You have been faithful in handling this small amount, so now I will give you many more responsibilities. Let's celebrate together!'"* and *"One who is faithful in a very little is also faithful in much, and one who is dishonest in a very little is also dishonest in much."* (Luke 16:10, ESV).

If you cannot steward your own heart and the little things, you can easily misuse influence over others and can be unfaithful in stewarding the larger things. If you cannot rule your own thoughts, external authority will feel overwhelming. God establishes kingship from the inside out, which is why identity matters so deeply, *"For as he thinketh in his heart, so is he"* (Proverbs 23:7, KJV). Authority without identity becomes tyranny. Identity without authority becomes frustration.

True kingship flows from knowing who you are and Whose you are. Jesus modeled this; He did not grasp for authority, He walked in it naturally because He knew where He came from and where He was going. His authority was calm, unforced, and unmistakable.

Kingship in God's kingdom looks like this:

- Responsibility without ego.
- Confidence without arrogance.
- Strength expressed through service.
- Authority exercised through love.

When we understand authority as stewardship, we stop asking, *"What am I allowed to do?"* and start asking, *"What has God entrusted me to do?"*

This shift changes everything.

- We stop waiting for permission to act because we know what the Father wants us to do.
- We stop shrinking back when obedience feels costly.
- We stop assuming someone else will carry responsibility we were meant to bear.

To be a king is not to live above others, it is to live answerable to God for how we represent Him.

You are not necessarily called to rule the world, but you are most certainly called to steward *your* world and stewardship begins with faithfulness in what is already in your hands. This is not pressure; it is power, in Christ. God would not entrust authority to someone He did not trust. He would not call you a king if He did not intend for you to walk with responsibility and courage. *"For if, by the trespass of the one man, death reigned through that one man, how much more will those who receive God's abundant provision of grace and of the gift of righteousness reign in life through the one man, Jesus Christ!"* (Romans 5:17, NIV).

Kingship is not about status. It is about stewardship. It is not about control, but about standing firm in doing what is right and bringing glory to the Kingdom of God, *"Therefore, put on the complete armor of God, so that you will be able to [successfully] resist and stand your ground in the evil day [of danger], and having done everything [that the crisis demands], to stand firm [in your place, fully prepared, immovable, victorious].* (Ephesians 6:13, AMP).

When authority is rooted in identity and love, it becomes a place of freedom rather than fear. It becomes a place of confidence, not pride. It becomes a place of certainty in times of challenge and a place of quiet in times of chaos.

Reflection Questions:
Kings: Authority & Stewardship

1. When you hear the word authority, what emotions or assumptions surface for you; comfort, resistance, fear, confusion? Where do you think those reactions come from?

2. Have you ever equated authority with control, dominance, or pride? How does the idea of authority as *stewardship* challenge or reshape that view?

3. In what areas of your life do you tend to see yourself as powerless rather than responsible? How might that perception be limiting what God has entrusted to you?

4. The chapter suggests that authority is exercised inwardly before it is ever exercised outwardly. What thoughts, attitudes, or responses might God be inviting you to steward more intentionally?

5. Where do you currently have influence, whether you recognize it or not?
   (Consider your home, relationships, workplace, church, or inner life.)

6. How do you usually respond when circumstances feel unfair, overwhelming, or out of your control? What might it look like to respond as a king who *stands* rather than withdraws?

7. Have you ever avoided responsibility because you feared failure or blame? How does knowing your authority flows from identity, not performance, change that fear?

8. Jesus modeled authority that was calm, grounded, and secure. What would need to shift in your view of yourself to live with that kind of steadiness?

9. What has God already placed in your hands; gifts, opportunities, relationships, or responsibilities, that you may have been waiting for "permission" to steward faithfully?

10. Sit quietly with this question:
    "What does faithful stewardship look like in my life right now?"
    Write down one area where God may be inviting you to stand with courage and responsibility.

Kingship does not begin with ruling others, it begins with faithful stewardship of what God has already entrusted to you. As you continue, consider how authority is meant to be balanced by intimacy with God, because authority without intimacy becomes dangerous and intimacy without responsibility becomes stagnant.

Chapter 7:
Priests: Access & Intercession

If kingship answers how we steward authority, priesthood answers how we remain anchored to God while doing so. If kingship teaches us how to stand, priesthood teaches us where to stand.

- ❖ Kings represent God's rule in the world.
- ❖ Priests represent God's presence to the world and the world back to God.

In Scripture, priests were not defined by productivity, but by where they were permitted to go and what they were called to do. Their calling was rooted in access. They were invited into places others could not enter, not because they were better, but because they were chosen. Priesthood has never been about earning closeness to God. It has always been about receiving it. Through Christ, access is no longer restricted. The barrier has been removed. The invitation stands open, not for a select few, but for all who belong to Him. To be a priest, then, is to live from proximity. " *19Therefore, brothers and sisters, since we have confidence to enter the Most Holy Place by the blood of Jesus, 20 by a new and living way opened for us through the curtain, that is, his body,* [21] *and since we have a great priest over the house of God,* [22] *let us draw near to God with a sincere heart and with the full assurance that faith brings, having our hearts sprinkled to cleanse us from a guilty conscience and having our bodies washed with pure water."* (Hebrews 10:19-22, NIV).

Many believers live as though God is distant, approachable only in crisis or formality. We treat prayer like an appointment instead of a relationship. However, priesthood reminds us that closeness is not the exception; it is the norm. We are not visitors in God's presence. We are residents.

Access changes everything.

- When you know you are welcome, you stop hiding.
- When you know you belong, you stop striving.
- When you know you are heard, you stop shouting.

Priesthood does not end with access, it flows into intercession. Scripture tells us *"the Spirit Himself intercedes for us"* (Romans 8:26). Intercession is participation, not pressure. To intercede is not merely to pray for others; it is to carry them before God with love, compassion, and faith. It is to stand in the space between heaven and earth, knowing that God cares deeply about what burdens His people. Intercession is not driven by obligation. It is born out of intimacy. We intercede not because we must, but because we have been close enough to God to trust His heart for others. We pray boldly because we know the One we are praying to. Priests do not manipulate outcomes, but rather they partner with God's purposes. *"Let us then approach God's throne of grace with confidence"* (Hebrews 4:16). Confidence does not come from performance, it comes from relationship.

This is why priesthood must accompany kingship. Scripture reminds us, *"But you are a chosen people, a royal priesthood, a holy nation, God's special possession, that you may declare the praises of him who called you out of darkness into his wonderful light."* (1 Peter 2:9). Priesthood is not a role for the few; it is the inheritance of all who belong to Christ. Authority without prayer becomes self-reliance.

Responsibility without intimacy becomes exhaustion. However, when kingship and priesthood are held together, authority is exercised with humility and strength.

Jesus modeled this life of intimacy and intercession. *"Very early in the morning, while it was still dark, Jesus got up… and prayed"* (Mark 1:35). He withdrew to pray, not because He lacked power or was unclear on direction, but because intimacy was important. He carried the needs of others to the Father and He carried the Father's heart back to the people. That is priesthood. To live as a priest means we do not disconnect from God when life becomes demanding, we return to Him. We remain rooted in presence, so that our actions flow from communion rather than pressure. It also means we do not retreat inward and ignore the world's pain. True priesthood is not escapism, it is engagement and encouragement, *"Be still, and know that I am God"* (Psalm 46:10).

- We carry others before God.
- We carry God's compassion back to others.

This is not reserved for the spiritually elite, it is the inheritance of every believer. Priesthood reminds us that we are never meant to carry authority alone. We are sustained by access, shaped by intimacy, and empowered by intercession.

- ❖ Kingship gives us responsibility.
- ❖ Priesthood gives us dependence.

Together, they form a life that is both grounded and guided; firmly rooted in God's presence and faithfully engaged in His purposes.

Reflection Questions:
Priests: Access & Intercession

1. When you think about being in God's presence, do you experience it more as welcome or as something you must earn? What has shaped that expectation?

2. The chapter says that priesthood is rooted in access, not performance. Where in your spiritual life do you still feel pressure to "do enough" before coming close to God?

3. How do you typically respond when life becomes demanding or overwhelming; do you withdraw from God, rush past Him, or return to Him?

4. Do you view prayer more as a task to complete or a place to dwell? How might that perspective be affecting your relationship with God?

5. What would change if you truly believed you are a *resident* in God's presence rather than a visitor?

6. Intercession is described as carrying others before God with compassion. Who has God placed on your heart that you may have been carrying alone instead of bringing into His presence?

7. Have you ever avoided praying for others because you doubted whether your prayers mattered? How does knowing you have access reshape that doubt?

8. How does intimacy with God sustain you differently than self-reliance or spiritual effort?

9. In what ways might your authority as a king be strengthened, not diminished, by dependence on God as a priest?

10. Sit quietly and reflect on this question:
    "Where is God inviting me to return to His presence; not to do more, but to remain?"
    Write down any thoughts, invitations, or resistance that surface.

Priests remind us that authority is sustained by intimacy. As you continue, consider what it means to live with both confidence and dependence; holding responsibility without losing closeness.

Chapter 8:
Holding the Crown and the Altar

Kingship and priesthood were never meant to be separated, Scripture declares that Jesus, *"formed us into a kingdom (a royal race), priests to His God and Father—to Him be the glory and the power and the majesty and the dominion throughout the ages and forever and ever. Amen (so be it)"* (Revelation 1:6).

From the beginning, God's design was not that His people would choose between authority and intimacy, action and presence, responsibility and dependence; His design was for us to choose it all and to live fully in what God calls us to. The crown and the altar belong together. When we hold only the crown, authority becomes heavy. We begin to rely on our own strength, measure success by outcomes, and carry responsibility without rest. Kingship without priesthood turns leadership into pressure.

When we hold only the altar, intimacy becomes inward. We remain close to God, but hesitant to engage the world. Priesthood without kingship turns devotion into retreat and God never intended for us to live in solitude. He told Adam and Eve to be fruitful and multiply, He wouldn't have said that if He only wanted one or two people on Earth and if we were to live in solitude. We are called to be in the world, no, not of it, but yes, in it. God does not want us to live in imbalance. We are called to stand in the world with authority while remaining rooted in God's presence. To steward what He has entrusted to us without drifting into self-reliance. To intercede without withdrawing and to act without striving.

This is the tension (and the beauty) of being both kings and priests. Jesus embodied this integration perfectly. He carried unquestioned authority, yet continually returned to the Father. He healed, taught, and confronted injustice, but He also withdrew to pray. *"All authority in heaven and on earth has been given to Me"* (Matthew 28:18) and yet *"He often withdrew to lonely places and prayed"* (Luke 5:16). His public strength was sustained by private communion. Jesus never used intimacy to avoid responsibility and He never used authority to bypass dependence.

That is the pattern we are invited into. Holding the crown and the altar means we do not measure our faithfulness by activity alone, nor by closeness alone. We allow God's presence to inform our decisions and we allow our obedience to flow from relationship. This integration requires attentiveness, thoughtfulness, and care; *"Unless the Lord builds the house, those who build it labor in vain"* (Psalm 127:1, ESV).

There will be seasons when responsibility presses hard and intimacy feels quiet. There will be moments when prayer feels rich and action feels daunting. The call is not perfection, it is alignment.

- ❖ When authority begins to exhaust you, return to the altar.
- ❖ When intimacy begins to isolate you, return to the crown.

Neither is a failure. Both are invitations.

Holding both also reshapes how we see success and success is no longer about how much we accomplish or how spiritual we appear. It becomes about faithfulness, remaining rooted in God while stewarding what He has placed in our care. This is where steadfastness is formed; not in dramatic moments of triumph or devotion, but in the quiet, consistent choice to remain aligned, to stand firm without hardening, to draw near without withdrawing.

Kings and priests do not live reactive lives. They live anchored lives.

- They know who they are.
- They know where they belong.
- They know Who sustains them.

Holding the crown and the altar does not mean life will be easy. It means it will be ordered and focused on carrying out the plans and purposes that God has ordained for you to carry out. Authority and intimacy working together create a life that is resilient, grounded, and free. This is not something you master, rather it is something you practice. Day-by-day, decision-by-decision, you learn to carry responsibility without losing closeness, and closeness without avoiding responsibility.

Remember:
- ❖ You were wanted.
- ❖ You were intentional.
- ❖ You are known and named.
- ❖ You are entrusted with authority.
- ❖ You are invited into intimacy.

Now you are called to hold them together.

Reflection Questions:
Holding the Crown & the Altar

1. As you reflect on kingship and priesthood together, which do you naturally lean toward; authority and action, or intimacy and withdrawal? Why do you think that is?

2. Have there been seasons in your life where you held the crown without returning to the altar; carrying responsibility without rest or dependence? What did that produce in you?

3. Have there been seasons where you stayed at the altar, but avoided the crown; remaining close to God while hesitating to step into responsibility? What fears or hesitations were present?

4. How do you currently measure faithfulness: by how much you do, or by how close you feel to God? How might God be inviting you to redefine faithfulness as alignment instead?

5. The chapter suggests returning to the altar when authority exhausts you, and returning to the crown when intimacy isolates you. Which invitation do you sense God extending to you right now?

6. What practices help you remain rooted in God's presence while engaging fully with the responsibilities of your life? Which practices might need to be strengthened or reclaimed?

7. In moments of pressure or decision-making, do you tend to act first and pray later, or pray without acting? What would it look like to hold both together?

8. How might your view of success change if success were
    defined by steadiness and faithfulness rather than
    outcomes or intensity?

9. What does an "anchored life" look like for you
    personally; one that is neither reactive nor withdrawn?

10. Sit quietly with this question:
    **"Where is my life out of alignment and what small
    adjustment is God inviting me to make?"**
    Write down what comes to mind, trusting that alignment
    often begins with gentle course correction.

Holding the crown and the altar is not a one-time decision, but a
daily posture. As you continue, consider what it means to remain
steadfast; firmly fixed in who you are, no matter what comes.

Part III: Formation

Understanding identity and embracing calling is not enough.

The deeper question is this: *How do you remain steady when life presses against what you believe?* Formation is where identity is tested and strengthened. It is where truth moves from inspiration to integration.

These chapters focus on becoming steadfast, firmly fixed in who God says you are, even when circumstances attempt to renegotiate that truth. Formation is not about intensity or perfection. It is about consistency. It is about returning again and again to what is true.

Here, you will learn what it means to hold both crown and altar; to carry responsibility without losing intimacy, and to remain anchored without withdrawing.

A life rooted in identity and aligned with calling does not avoid storms. It stands through them.

This is where resilience is formed.

Chapter 9:
Steadfast and Firmly Fixed

Before closing we must address the question: How do I remain anchored in this identity when life presses, shakes, or wounds me? Identity that is not anchored will always be negotiated, swayed, forgotten, or overlooked. It will shift with circumstances, rise and fall with emotion, and weaken under pressure. That is why Scripture does not merely invite us to know who we are, it calls us to remain steadfast and firmly fixed. Steadfastness is not intensity, rather it is stability.

To be firmly fixed is to be rooted deeply enough that life cannot uproot you. Throughout this journey, we have returned again and again to one truth: you are valuable and that identity precedes everything else. Before you act, before you lead, before you endure, you must know who you are.

However, knowing is not the same as remaining. Many believers encounter moments of clarity, revelation, encouragement, and spiritual insight; only to lose their footing when hardship comes. The problem is not that the truth was wrong, it is that the truth was not yet anchored. Steadfastness is the practice of returning and remaining firmly fixed, no matter the storms that come. It is choosing, again and again, to stand on what God has said; even when feelings disagree, circumstances contradict, or progress feels slow.

You will face moments that test everything you believe.

- Moments when obedience feels costly.
- Moments when prayers feel unanswered.
- Moments when identity feels fragile and old narratives try to resurface.

In those moments, steadfastness matters more than certainty.

To remain firmly fixed is to refuse to renegotiate who you are based on what you are experiencing.

- You are still wanted, even when you feel rejected.
- You are still intentional, even when your path feels unclear.
- You are still known and named, even when you feel overlooked.
- You are still a king, even when you feel powerless.
- You are still a priest, even when God feels quiet.

Steadfastness does not deny pain, but it does deny pain of the authority to define truth.

This is where kingship and priesthood fully mature. Kings remain steady under pressure. They do not abandon responsibility when circumstances shift. They stand, not because it is easy, but because they are rooted. Priests remain close even when silence stretches on. They do not withdraw from God when answers feel delayed. They remain, not because they understand everything, but because they trust His presence.

Steadfastness is where authority and intimacy are tested and proven. It is also where humility deepens. Not the humility of self-erasure, but the humility of trust. The quiet confidence that says, *"I will remain, even here."* Being firmly fixed does not mean you never doubt, it means doubt does not have the final word. It does not mean you never stumble, it means you return to truth more quickly than you used to.

Roots grow underground before anything visible appears and much of what God is establishing in you will not be immediately apparent to others or even to you. However, things being unseen does not mean there is nothing happening. What is firmly fixed beneath the surface will eventually support the fruit above it. This is why consistency matters more than intensity.

- Daily returning.
- Daily choosing truth.
- Daily aligning crown and altar.

Not perfectly. Faithfully.

Steadfast people are not impressive because they are unshaken, they are compelling because they are anchored.

- They do not live reactive lives.
- They do not chase every voice.
- They do not abandon themselves under pressure.

They know who they are and that knowing has settled into the fabric of their being.

To be steadfast is to live from knowing your identity in Christ, rather than feeling that you must strive for perfection to obtain that identity. It means to stop striving for assurance and begin standing in it. This is the invitation you are left with; not to try harder, but to remain.

- Remain in truth.
- Remain in love.
- Remain in responsibility.
- Remain in presence.

You were not created for a moment of belief, you were created for a life firmly fixed in who God says you are and that kind of life; quietly rooted, deeply anchored, faithfully aligned, will stand no matter what comes

Reflection Questions:
Steadfast & Firmly Fixed

1. When life becomes difficult or uncertain, what do you most often find yourself renegotiating: your worth, God's goodness, or your identity? Why?

2. How do you typically respond when what you believe conflicts with what you feel or experience?

3. The chapter distinguishes between *knowing* truth and *remaining* in it. Where have you experienced moments of clarity that later felt difficult to hold onto?

4. What circumstances or pressures tend to shake your sense of identity the most?

5. How has your understanding of yourself shifted from the beginning of this book until now?

6. Which truth feels most important for you to remain firmly fixed in during this season of your life?

7. Steadfastness is described as the practice of returning. Where in your life do you sense an invitation to return: to truth, to trust, to presence, or to responsibility?

8. How might your life look different if consistency mattered more to you than intensity?

9. What practices help you stay anchored when emotions, fear, or disappointment arise? Which of those need to be strengthened or protected?

10. Sit quietly with this statement and reflect on it honestly: **"I am firmly fixed in who God says I am."** What feels solid? What still feels tender?

Take a moment to look back at your answers throughout these chapters. Notice the progression. Identity forms slowly and strengthens over time. You are not meant to rush this, you are meant to contemplate, think on, and constantly grow in a greater understanding of who you are and how valuable you are to the King of kings.

Epilogue:
Walking Forward as Kings and Priests

This book does not end with certainty, rather it ends with invitation.

You will not walk forward with every question answered or every struggle resolved. That was never the goal. What you carry forward instead is something deeper and more enduring: identity that has taken root.

- ❖ You are wanted.
- ❖ You are intentional.
- ❖ You are known and named.
- ❖ You are entrusted with authority.
- ❖ You are invited into intimacy.

Now, you are called to walk forward as both king and priest; not occasionally, not ideally, but daily.

Walking as a king does not mean you dominate your life or master every outcome. It means you take responsibility for what God has placed within your reach. You steward your thoughts, your words, your influence, and your choices with courage and integrity. You stand when it would be easier to shrink back. You remain faithful when circumstances are unclear.

Walking as a priest does not mean you retreat from the world into spiritual isolation. It means you remain close to God while staying engaged with others. You return to presence when life becomes demanding. You carry people, situations, and burdens into prayer; not as a last resort, but as a way of life.

You will have days when the crown feels heavy, return to the altar. You will have days when the altar feels quiet, return to the crown. Neither posture replaces the other, together, they form a life that is balanced, resilient, and free. There will be moments when old voices try to rename you, when fear, shame, or exhaustion whisper that you are still the person you used to be. When that happens, remember: identity does not reset with emotion. You do not lose who you are because life becomes hard. You do not walk forward to *become* a king and a priest, you walk forward in the confident assurance that you *are* a king and a priest.

- Your authority is not loud.
- Your intimacy is not fragile.
- Your calling is not theoretical.

It is lived out in ordinary faithfulness; in the way you respond instead of react, in the way you choose truth over fear, in the way you carry responsibility without losing tenderness, and in the way you remain anchored when life shifts.

You are not alone in this calling.

- The same God who wanted you walks with you.
- The same God who named you sustains you.
- The same God who entrusted you empowers you.

Remember, He is patient, He is kind, He is loving, and He created you in His image. This is not about getting it right every time. It is about returning, again and again, to who you are and where you belong. As you walk forward, do so without apology.

- You are not an afterthought in God's story. You are a beloved child.

- You are not merely tolerated. You are firmly fixed.
- You are not provisional. You are a king and a priest.

The life ahead of you is not about proving that identity, it is about living from it.

- Go forward rooted.
- Go forward steady.
- Go forward as who you already are.

Thank You for Reading

If this book encouraged you or helped you see your identity in Christ more clearly, would you consider leaving a brief review wherever you purchased it?

Reviews help other readers discover books like this and allow the message to reach people who may need it. Even a short sentence about what you found meaningful is deeply appreciated.

Also, if this message resonated with you, please consider sharing it with a friend, small group, or someone who might need encouragement. Sometimes the truths that change us are the same truths someone else is quietly searching for.

Further books are to come, so keep your eyes open for the next one!

Thank you for being part of the journey.

About the Author

Born and raised in the beautiful islands of Hawaii, Tiffany K. Grainger is passionate about helping others understand their identity in Christ and live faithfully from that foundation. Through teaching and writing, she encourages believers to grow in spiritual confidence, responsibility, and intimacy with God.

Tiffany has dedicated her life to serving others and creating meaningful impact across the globe. A graduate of Colorado State University-Pueblo, she began her career as a police officer in the New York City Police Department, serving in the South Bronx. Her passion for justice eventually led her to India, where she worked to combat human trafficking and empower vulnerable communities.

With a deep commitment to helping others heal and thrive, Tiffany earned her Master's in Public Administration and her Doctorate in Biblical Counseling. She also serves her community through working in law enforcement, bringing her vast experience and unwavering dedication to her role in public service.

In addition to her work in law enforcement, Tiffany is a devoted educator, sharing her knowledge and expertise as a professor, where she inspires the next generation of leaders. She is also the President of the Board of Directors for Oasis USA, an organization committed to ending human trafficking.

Additionally, Tiffany channels her entrepreneurial spirit into running a successful restaurant alongside her husband. Together, they've created a warm and welcoming space for their community while raising their two wonderful children.

Whether she's reading, horseback riding, camping, traveling, or enjoying quality time with her family, Tiffany finds joy in life's simple pleasures. An adventurer at heart, Tiffany is also a licensed private pilot. Her journey is a testament to the power of resilience, service, and a deep-seated belief in the ability to create change: one life, one community, and one moment at a time.

This book was written from a desire to help readers move beyond uncertainty about their worth and calling, and into a grounded understanding of who they are before God.